EASY

EGG BITES

COOKBOOK

Quick,Easy and Delicious Egg Bites Recipes for the
Perfect Weight Loss

Louis Aronne

Warning-Disclaimer

This " EASY EGG BITES COOKBOOK" aims to give people ideas about egg bites recipes. We can not ensure that everyone will be successful by following the book.

GRATITUDE

Farhan Fuad Sadi

(Editor and illustrator)

From_Bangladesh

I must begin by expressing my gratitude to this gentleman. About web publications, I am a newcomer in this field. So, it was challenging for me to publish my first book online. Farhan assists me greatly. Moreover, he designs my book superbly. I am appreciative of him.

Thanks again.

Louis Aronne

Contents

INTRODUCTION

Egg bites are a popular breakfast dish that originated in the United States. They combine eggs, cheese, and other ingredients, baked in a muffin tin, to create a small, portable breakfast item that is easy to grab and go.

The basic recipe for egg bites typically includes eggs, cheese, and meat or vegetables. The eggs are beaten and combined with the other ingredients, then poured into a muffin tin and baked until the egg is fully cooked. Some popular add-ins for egg bites include bacon, ham, sausage, spinach, mushrooms, and bell peppers.

Egg bites have become increasingly popular in recent years because they are a great low-carb, high-protein breakfast option. They are also highly customizable, making them a versatile breakfast option tailored to individual tastes and dietary needs.

Egg bites can be served hot or cold and are often enjoyed as a grab-and-go breakfast option. They can be reserved in the refrigerator for several days and reheated quickly in the microwave, making them a convenient and healthy breakfast option for busy mornings.

HISTORY OF EGG BITES

Egg bites, also known as sous vide eggs, are a popular breakfast food recently gaining popularity. The dish consists of eggs that are beaten with cheese, cream, and other ingredients, then cooked in sous vide water bath.

The origins of egg bites are partially transparent, but it is believed that the dish first gained popularity in the USA in the 2010s. One of the earliest iterations of the dish was the Starbucks Sous Vide Egg Bites, which were introduced in 2017 and quickly became a customer favorite.

The popularity of egg bites can be attributed to several factors:

1. They are a convenient and easy-to-prepare breakfast option that can be made earlier and reheated as needed.
2. They are lofty in protein and low in carbs, making them a popular choice for people following a low-carb or ketogenic diet.
3. They are highly customizable, allowing home cooks to experiment with different ingredients and flavor combinations.

Today, egg bites are a popular breakfast food found on the menus of many restaurants and coffee shops and in home kitchens worldwide.

WHY EGG BITES

Egg bites have become popular because they are a quick and effortless way to make a protein-packed breakfast or snack. They are typically made by blending eggs with other ingredients such as cheese, vegetables, or meats, then pouring the mixture into small molds and baking or cooking in a water bath.

There are several reasons why egg bites have become so popular. First, they are convenient and portable, making them an ideal breakfast or snack option for people on the go. They can be made and stored in the fridge or freezer for easy meal prep.

Second, egg bites are versatile food items that can be customized to fit various tastes and dietary preferences. They can be made with different fillings, such as spinach and feta, bacon and cheddar, or ham and broccoli. Additionally, they can be made keto, paleo, or gluten-free by simply swapping out ingredients.

Finally, egg bites are a healthy food option. They are high in protein, which can assist in keeping you feeling full and satisfied, and they can be made with healthy ingredients such as vegetables, herbs, and spices.

HOW TO PROPERLY WHISK THE EGGS

Whisking eggs properly is an essential skill for many recipes, and it can make a big difference in the texture and appearance of your final dish. Here's how to do it:

Start by cracking the eggs into a mixing bowl. If you're making a recipe that screams for only egg whites or yolks, separate the eggs first.

Use a whisk to beat the eggs vigorously, breaking up the yolks and whites and combining them thoroughly. The goal is to create a consistent mixture without any streaks or lumps.

To add air to the mixture, whisk the eggs for a few minutes until they become pale and frothy. This is particularly important for recipes like omelets and soufflés, which require light and airy eggs.

If you're whisking the eggs for a recipe that calls for a specific consistency, like a custard or a cake, pay attention to the instructions and whisk the eggs for the recommended time.

When you're finished whisking, clean your whisk and bowl thoroughly with hot, soapy water to avoid cross-contamination.

The key to whisking eggs properly is to be patient, thorough, and consistent in your technique. With a bit of practice, you'll be capable of achieving perfectly whisked eggs every time!

Boiling Time:

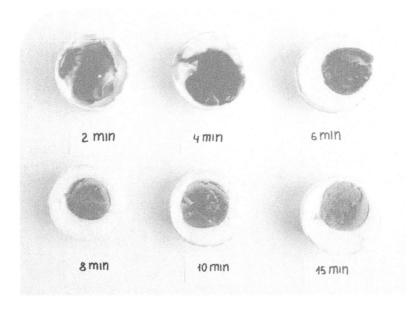

The boiling time for eggs can vary depending on the preferred level of doneness and the size of the egg. Here are some general guidelines:
1. Soft-boiled eggs (runny yolk): 4-6 minutes

2. Medium-boiled eggs (partially runny yolk): 7-9 minutes
3. Hard-boiled eggs (fully cooked yolk): 12-15 minutes.

It's important to note that the boiling time may need to be adjusted slightly depending on the altitude you are at, as higher altitudes can affect the boiling temperature of the water. Additionally, using a timer or watching the clock closely is a good idea to ensure that the eggs are not overcooked or undercooked.

EASY OVEN EGG BITE RECIPE

Prep: 12 mins Cook:20 mins Total: 32 mins
Servings: 6 servings
Yield: 12-13 egg bites

Ingredients

- cooking spray
- eight large eggs
- 1 cup shredded cheddar cheese
- 1/2 cup coarsely chopped packed baby spinach
- 1/3 cup half-and-half milk
- 2/3 cup diced tomatoes
- 1/3 cup thinly sliced green onions
- one dash of freshly ground black pepper
- 1/4 teaspoon salt

Steps:

Arrange the components. The oven must be heated to 350 degrees with a rack in the middle. Cooking spray should be used on a 12-well muffin pan.

Shaved cheese, half-and-half, salt, pepper, and nutmeg must be combined with the eggs in a big bowl. Stir in the spinach, green onions, and chopped tomatoes.

About 1/4 cup of the mixture should be placed in each muffin cup when you spread it evenly. Bake for 18 mins or until they are crisp, fluffy, and gently golden.

Recipe Variations

Quiche Lorraine-Style Egg Bites: Leave out the tomatoes and the spinach. Substitute the cheddar with 3/4 cup of finely shredded Gruyére cheese and 1/4 cup of Parmesan cheese, and then stir in 1/2 cup of chopped cooked bacon (approximately 6 to 8 pieces), 1/3 cup of sliced green onions, and a pinch of nutmeg.

How to Store and Freeze

Eat the egg bites you've refrigerated in a closed container within four days after they've cooled.

Place any leftover egg bites on a baking sheet and freeze them. Place the whole baking sheet in the refrigerator for one to two hours or until it becomes solid. For up to two months, freeze the frozen egg bites in a knot-freezer bag. The egg bites will thaw in the fridge overnight.

Egg bites may be cooked again in the microwave for 20 to 30 seconds or by putting them in a baking dish and heating them for 10 minutes in a heated oven and set to 350 degrees Fahrenheit.

Nutrition Facts (per serving):

Calories-130 Fat-10g Carbs-2g Protein-10g

SPINACH FETA EGG WHITE BITES

Prep Time: 5 minutes Cook Time: 12-15 minutes Total Time: 17-20 minutes

Yield: 12

Description

These simple egg white bites, baked in a muffin tin, are filled with baby spinach, feta, chives, and roasted tomatoes or red peppers.

Ingredients

- Nonstick cooking spray
- 1–16 ounce carton of egg whites (2 cups)
- 1/2 cup milk
- one teaspoon of kosher salt
- 1/2 teaspoon black pepper
- 2 cups baby spinach
- 1/2 cup chopped jarred roasted tomatoes or roasted red peppers
- 1/3 cup crumbled feta
- two tablespoons minced chives

Instructions

Set the oven to 350 degrees Fahrenheit. Spray nonstick cooking spray in a 12-cup muffin pan. Mix the egg whites, milk, salt, and pepper in a bowl.

Divide chopped roasted tomatoes (red peppers) and spinach into each muffin cup. Add egg whites until about three-quarters of the way filled, then top with crumbled feta and chives.

The white egg bites should be baked for 12 to 15 minutes or until set. To remove the cups from the pan as needed, run a paring knife around them.

Notes

Store leftover bits in the refrigerator for five days in an airtight container. Wolf down them cold on their own, with cooked grains or a salad. Leftovers are best not heated up. Let them warm up if you'd rather have them at room temperature than freezing.

You can use nine entire eggs in place of egg whites. 15 to 20 minutes should be added to the cooking time. Feta cheese can be replaced with goat cheese.

MINI QUICHE BREAKFAST BITES

Preparation Time: 22-25 mins Cook Time: 25 mins
Additional Time: 5-7 mins Total Time: 55 mins

Ingredients

- cooking spray
- Eight large eggs
- ½ cup heavy cream
- ½ teaspoon dried dill weed
- ½ teaspoon hot mustard powder
- salt and ground black pepper to taste
- 1 cup shredded Swiss cheese

- 1 cup cubed fully cooked ham
- ½ cup diced onion (Optional)
- One tablespoon of chopped roasted red peppers

Directions

Set the oven to 175 degrees C. Put cooking spray into 36 miniature muffin tins.

In a bowl, whisk together the cream and eggs. Salt, pepper, mustard powder, and dill are all used. Add Swiss cheese, ham, onion, and peppers in limited quantities. Pour one spoonful of batter into each muffin cup that has been prepared.

Bake in the preheated oven for about 16-a8 minutes, or until the center is placed and the top is lightly browned. Before serving, let cool for five minutes.

EASY PESTO EGG MUFFINS

Prep Time: 3-5 minutes
Cook Time 25 minutes
Total Time 30 minutes
Servings 12

Ingredients

- One tablespoon butter
- One yellow onion, diced (about 2 cups)
- 1 cup cremini mushrooms, diced (or other mushrooms)
- One red bell pepper, diced

- 1 cup packed spinach, chopped
- Eight large eggs
- ¼ cup milk
- Three tablespoons pesto
- ¾ teaspoon fine sea salt
- ¼ teaspoon black pepper
- ⅔ cup crumbled feta cheese

Instructions

Preheat: Preheat oven to 350°F (177°C).

Cook veggies:
1. Melt butter in a skillet on high heat.
2. Include onion, and cook until softened, about 3 minutes.
3. Add mushrooms and red pepper.
4. Cook until onion is golden brown and mushrooms are softened, about 5 minutes.
5. Stir in spinach, and cook until it begins to wilt, about 1 minute.
6. Remove from heat.

Whisk eggs: In a large bowl, whisk together eggs, milk, pesto, salt, and pepper.

Assemble:
1. Lightly spray a muffin pan or line it with paper cups (see note 1).
2. Divide veggies into the cups, then sprinkle with feta.
3. Pour egg mixture on top.

Bake: Bake until the eggs are set in the middle, about 18 minutes. Let cool slightly, then lift from the pan. Cover and refrigerate extras (see note 2).

Notes

Paper muffin cups: If you prefer to line the muffin pan (rather than spray it), choose parchment / nonstick muffin cups so the paper doesn't stick to the eggs.
Storage tips:
1. If you use paper muffin cups, peel them off before refrigerating (otherwise, they can accumulate moisture).
2. Refrigerate egg muffins in an airtight container for 3 to 4 days.
3. Reheat in the oven, or eat cold.

BREAKFAST EGG MUFFINS WITH BACON AND SPINACH

PREP TIME-20 mins
COOK TIME-25 mins
TOTAL TIME-45 mins

Ingredients

- Six eggs
- ¼ cup milk
- ¼ teaspoon salt
- 2 cups cheddar cheese shredded
- about 8 oz fresh spinach cooked and drained
- Six bacon slices cooked
- ½ cup Parmesan cheese shredded

Instructions

Preheat oven to 350 degrees. Use a regular 12-cup muffin pan. Spray the whole muffin pan with nonstick cooking spray.

In a bowl, beat eggs until smooth. Add milk, salt, and Cheddar cheese and mix. Stir spinach-cooked bacon into the egg mixture.

Fill the muffin tins with greased egg mixture to the 3/4 level.

Add some grated Parmesan cheese to each muffin cup. Bake for 25 minutes. Please stay away from the oven, and allow the muffins to cool for 30 minutes before taking them from the pan.

SCRAMBLED EGG MUFFIN CUPS

Prep Time: 15 mins
Cook Time: 30 mins
Total Time: 45 mins

Equipment

- Glass Measuring Bowl
- Measuring Cups
- Mixing Bowl

Ingredients

- ½ pound bulk pork sausage
- 12 eggs
- ½ cup chopped onion
- ½ cup chopped green bell pepper, or to taste
- ½ teaspoon salt
- ¼ teaspoon ground black pepper
- ¼ teaspoon garlic powder
- ½ cup shredded Cheddar cheese

Directions

Set the oven to 350 degrees Fahrenheit (175 degrees C). Twelve muffin tins should be lightly greased or lined with paper liners.

A big skillet should be heated at medium-high. Sausage is added and cooked for 10 to 15 minutes until crumbly, uniformly browned, and no longer pink. The grease should be drained.

In a large basin, beat the eggs. Salt, garlic powder, onion, and green pepper are combined. Cheese and sausage should be combined. Into the prepared muffin cups, spoon.

Bake for 20 to 25 minutes in the preheated oven or until a knife inserted close to the center comes out clean.

CHEDDAR CHIVE EGG BITES

Yield: 24 egg bites
Prep: 10 minutes
Cook: 13 minutes
Total: 23 minutes

Ingredients

- Eight large eggs
- Three tablespoons of milk (any type will work)
- 1 1/2 tablespoons minced fresh chives (sub: fresh basil or parsley)
- 1/4 teaspoon salt
- 1/8 teaspoon pepper
- 4–5 pieces of cooked uncured bacon, chopped into bite-sized pieces

- 1 cup shredded cheddar cheese

Instructions

Make It Now:
Preheat the oven to 350°F. Generously grease a mini muffin pan. If using a silicone pan, placing it on a baking sheet is a good idea.
Whisk together the eggs, milk, chives, salt, and pepper in a glass measuring cup with a spout.
Fill each muffin cup with the egg mixture, gently pouring until it is around 3/4 full. Divide the bacon and cheese equally among the muffin cups, then top with both.

Bake on the center rack for about 13 minutes or until the eggs are in the middle. Remove to a cooling rack and let cool for a few minutes. Run a butter knife around the sides of each egg bite and gently remove each one to the cooling rack.

Keep cold for up to 5 days in the refrigerator in an airtight container. Heat in the microwave for 10 seconds at a time for later use. Overcooking them will cause them to become rubbery.

Freeze For Later: Fully cook and cool the egg bites. Package them in a single layer in a freezer bag and try to remove as much air as possible from the pack. Here are two ways to remove air from a bag without a vacuum sealer. Or, you can freeze them in an airtight container, dividing layers with parchment paper. Place a layer of plastic wrap or foil over them inside the container.

Prepare From Frozen: Thaw in the fridge for a few hours, preferably. However, if you don't have time, you can briefly thaw using the microwave's defrost setting. To rewarm, wrap egg bites in a moist paper towel and microwave in very short increments until warmed through. Don't overcook them while reheating!

RITZ STEAKHOUSE BITES

Prep Time: 15 mins
Cook Time: 15 mins
Total Time: 30 mins

Ingredients

Creamed Spinach:
- Two teaspoons of olive oil
- 1 (6-ounce) package of baby spinach leaves
- One tablespoon butter
- One tablespoon of minced shallots
- ½ teaspoon nutmeg
- Two tablespoons heavy cream
- ⅛ teaspoon salt
- Pinch of black pepper

Béarnaise Sauce:
- One tablespoon butter
- Two tablespoons minced shallots
- One tablespoon of white wine vinegar
- One egg yolk

- One tablespoon of lemon juice
- ½ cup melted butter
- 18 RITZ Crackers
- 3 ounces thinly sliced, cooked beef tenderloin, but into bite-sized pieces

Directions

Heat olive oil in saute pan over medium heat. Add spinach and cover for 1 minute to steam. Uncover and stir spinach until it is wilted. Drain spinach, dry between paper towels, and chop. Melt butter in the same pan over medium heat. Add shallots and saute for a minute. Add heavy cream and nutmeg; stir to combine. Add chopped spinach and mix thoroughly. Remove from heat when spinach is creamy. Add salt and pepper. Set aside.

Melt one tablespoon of butter in a separate saute pan; add shallots and white wine vinegar. Cook until all liquid has evaporated, about a minute. Remove from the pan; set aside to cool.
Add egg yolk and lemon juice to the blender; slowly blend in half a cup of melted butter until the smooth and creamy mixture is. Pour into shallots mixture. Stir in chopped fresh tarragon.

To assemble bites, place about 1-1/2 teaspoons of creamed spinach on top of a RITZ Cracker. Place a slice of steak on top of the creamed spinach, then drizzle 1-1/2 teaspoon bearnaise sauce over the steak.

CRISPY TOFU BITES

Prep Time: 10 mins
Cook Time: 10 mins
Additional Time: 15 mins
Total Time: 35 mins

Ingredients

- 1 (12-ounce) package of extra-firm tofu
- 1 cup self-rising flour
- Two tablespoons cornstarch
- One teaspoon salt
- One teaspoon of ground black pepper
- Two tablespoons vegetable oil, or as needed

Directions

The tofu must be drained, put on a platter, and covered with heavy plates to drain any moisture for about 15 minutes. Twenty-four bite-sized pieces must be cut out. Combine flour, salt, cornstarch, and pepper in a large plastic bag that can be sealed. In the bag with the tofu, pack it, and shake it to coat. Shaking off the extra flour mixture, transfer the tofu to a platter.
Oil must be added to a skillet and heated to almost smoke. Sauté tofu in heated oil for about 5 minutes on each side, often flipping, until golden brown on both sides.

Tips

Do not overload the skillet when frying the tofu; if necessary, cook in batches.

CHEESY CAULIFLOWER BREAKFAST EGG CUPS

yield: 4 servings

Prep time: 6 hrs 54 mins
Cook time: 20 mins
Total time: 40 mins

Ingredients

- 4 cups cauliflower florets
- Five eggs
- 1 cup shredded cheddar cheese
- ¼ cup basil, chopped
- 1 cup cherry tomatoes, halved
- ¼ tsp oregano, salt & pepper

Instructions

Preheat oven to 350°F (180°C). Process cauliflower until it's finely ground like couscous. In a bowl, whisk eggs. Add cheese and cauliflower. Mix to combine Season with salt, pepper, and oregano.

Lightly spray the muffin tin (I used mini muffin tins!) and fill it with the mixture. Decorate with basil leaves, cherry tomatoes, or your favorite toppings.

Bake for 15-20 minutes. Allow to cool, serve, and enjoy!

EGGPLANT PARMESAN BITES

Prep Time: 30 mins
Cook Time: 15 mins
Additional Time: 30 mins
Total Time: 1 hrs 15 mins

Ingredients

- One tablespoon of sea salt
- One small eggplant, cut into 1/2-inch rounds
- 1 cup Italian-seasoned bread crumbs
- One egg
- One teaspoon of olive oil, or more as needed
- ½ cup ricotta cheese
- 24 pita chips or more to taste
- 24 cherry tomatoes, or more to taste
- 24 basil leaves

Directions

Preheat oven to 190 degrees C. Sprinkle two teaspoons salt over eggplant rounds in a colander; allow to drain for at least 30 minutes. Rinse the salt off the eggplant.

Spread bread crumbs into a shallow bowl and beat the egg in a separate bowl. Dip eggplant into egg, allowing excess egg to drip off the eggplant; press into bread crumbs until eggplant slices are evenly coated on both sides.

Place the olive oil-coated eggplant on a baking sheet and arrange it as desired. For about 10 minutes, bake in the oven until barely browned. Mix the remaining one teaspoon of salt with ricotta cheese in a bowl. Spoon ricotta cheese mixture onto each eggplant.

Bake eggplant in the oven until cheese is heated through, 5 to 7 minutes. Place one eggplant slice onto each pita chip; top with a cherry tomato and basil leaf.

Cook's Note:

You can also use fresh mozzarella in place of the ricotta if desired. Crackers or toast rounds can be substituted for pita chips. If eggplant rounds are large, cut them in half, so the eggplant fits on your crackers.

EGG BITES WITH BACON & GRUYÈRE

Servings: 12 egg bites
Prep Time: 15 Minutes
Cook Time: 25 Minutes
Total Time: 40 Minutes

Ingredients

- Four slices bacon, diced
- Six large eggs
- 4% milk-fat cottage cheese
- 1¼ cups shredded Gruyère
- Two tablespoons cornstarch
- Heaping ¼ teaspoon salt
- ½ teaspoon hot sauce
- ⅛ teaspoon freshly ground black pepper

Instructions

Boil some water in a kettle. Place one oven rack in the middle and another in the bottom—the oven to 300 degrees Fahrenheit.

Put a 9x13-inch metal or ceramic baking sheet on the bottom rack and partially it with the kettle's boiling water. This will fill the oven with steam, allowing the egg bits to cook more slowly and develop a custardy texture.

Use a lot of nonstick cooking spray to cover a muffin pan. Cook the bacon, tossing regularly, in a small nonstick pan over medium-high heat for 5 to 6 minutes or until crisp. Transfer the bacon to a plate covered with towels using a slotted spoon so it can drain.

Eggs, cottage cheese, Gruyère, cornstarch, salt, pepper, and spicy sauce should be combined in a blender until the mixture is entirely smooth, about 30 seconds.

Each muffin pan well must be filled roughly three times with the egg mixture. Over the egg bites, evenly distribute the bacon. Press a small amount of the bacon into the batter with a spoon or your finger to prevent it from floating to the top. The eggs should be set on the center rack after 20 to 25 minutes of baking. The egg bits are done when the edges begin to peel away gently. When the egg pieces calm, some of them may settle and lose some of their inflated appearances.
The egg parts must be removed from the oven and allowed to cool in the pan for about five minutes. Use a spoon to carefully lift the egg pieces off the pan's lip and set them on a platter.

Serve hot.

Freezer-Friendly Instructions:

1. Store the chilled egg parts in an airtight jar for up to three days in the fridge.

2. Reheat for 60 to 90 seconds at 50% power in the microwave. The egg bits may also be stored in an airtight container for 2-3 months.

3. Reheat in the microwave after defrosting in the refrigerator for the night.

PESTO & GROUND BEEF BREAKFAST EGG BITES

Servings: 6
Prep time: 10 minutes
Cook time: 25 minutes
Total time: 35 minutes

Ingredients

- 7 Eggs
- 1 lb Laura's Lean Ground Beef
- 1/4 cup Unsweetened almond
- 1/2 cup Cherry tomatoes
- 1 Bell pepper
- 1/2 cup Pesto
- Cooking oil spray
- Salt, pepper, and garlic powder to taste

Preparation

One pound of Laura's Lean ground beef is pan-fried, diced, and seasoned with salt, pepper, and garlic powder. Set aside once cooked thoroughly.
Bell peppers and cherry tomatoes must be diced finely.

Set the oven to 350 degrees.
Spray cooking oil in a muffin pan that is not lined before putting the egg cups together. Each hole should contain a tiny scoop of cooked ground beef, pesto, cherry tomatoes, and bell peppers.
Add salt, pepper, and garlic powder to a bowl with seven eggs and milk. Fill each hole with ground beef, veggies, and egg mixture to almost the top.
Bake for 20–25 minutes at 350°F.
Serve with a warm cup of coffee for breakfast!

CRAB SWISS BITES

Prep Time: 10 mins
Cook Time: 12 mins
Total Time: 22 mins

Ingredients

- 6-ounce can of crabmeat drained and flaked
- One tablespoon sliced green onion
- ¼ cup shredded Swiss cheese
- ½ cup mayonnaise
- One teaspoon of lemon juice
- ¼ teaspoon curry powder
- 1 (8-ounce) package of dinner rolls
- 5-ounce can of water chestnuts

Directions

Preheat oven to 200 degrees C.
Mix crabmeat, green onion, Swiss cheese, lemon juice, mayonnaise, and curry powder in a medium bowl.

Separate dinner rolls into three pieces each. Spoon equal portions of the crabmeat mixture onto the roll pieces. Top with water chestnuts.

Bake in the oven for 10 to 12 minutes or until bubbly and golden brown.

FRIED VENISON BACKSTRAP

Prep Time: 30 mins
Cook Time: 20 mins
Additional Time: 1 hrs
Total Time: 1 hrs 50 mins

Ingredients

- 2-pound venison backstrap
- 2 ½ cups milk
- Two tablespoons of hot pepper sauce
- 3 cups vegetable oil for frying
- One tablespoon of ground black pepper
- 3 cups all-purpose flour
- Two tablespoons salt

- Two eggs

Directions

Slices of venison should be placed in a shallow bowl with 2 cups of milk and spicy sauce. Cover and marinate for an hour after stirring to coat.

Heat the vegetable oil to 320 degrees F. (165 degrees C) using an electric skillet or fryer.

Put together a dredging station: In a small bowl, combine the flour, salt, and pepper. Whisk the eggs and the remaining 1/2 cup of milk in another shallow bowl.

Slices of venison are dipped in flour mixture, then in egg mixture, and finally back into the flour mixture. Take away any extra flour. Around 3 minutes, fry in the heated oil until each side is lightly browned.

Before serving, remove with tongs and quickly pat it dry with paper towels.

EGG MUFFINS WITH CARAMELIZED ONIONS

Prep time-15 mins
Cook time-1 hr
Servings-4

Ingredients

- Ten eggs large
- One white onion medium
- 1/2 cup red bell pepper diced
- 1/2 cup button or cremini mushroom diced
- 1 cup spinach raw, chopped
- 4 oz white cheddar cheese shredded
- 2 Tbsp avocado oil
- Three sprays of avocado oil cooking spray

Instructions

Heat 1 Tbsp avocado oil in a large pan on medium-low heat, and add sliced onion when hot.
Cook onions on medium-low heat for approximately 30 minutes, until soft and browned, stirring every 5 mins.

Meanwhile, heat the oven to 350 degrees Fahrenheit and heat a second pan on medium heat.
Add the remaining 1 Tbsp avocado oil to the second pan, and add the diced bell pepper, mushrooms, and spinach to the pan when hot.

Saute vegetables for approximately 7-10 minutes until soft. Spray a silicone muffin tin with avocado oil cooking spray.

Add small spoonfuls of cooked veggies, caramelized onions, and a sprinkle of shredded white cheddar cheese to each tin.

Whisk all the eggs in a large bowl or measuring cup with a spout. Next, divide the mixture evenly among the muffin tins.

Bake at 350 for approximately 25-30 minutes. Check for doneness by inserting a knife into an egg muffin. Ensure eggs are completely set.

SOFT BOILED EGG BITES

Prep Time 2 minutes
Cook Time 6 minutes
Servings-7 egg bites

Ingredients

- Nine eggs
- 1/3 cup sour cream or yogurt
- 2 tbsp grated Parmesan or sharp cheddar
- 2 tsp chopped fresh basil
- Salt and pepper

Instructions

Use the baking spray to coat a 7-pocket egg bite mold. Once it's on the counter, put it on the trivet with the long handles. This makes lowering it inside the Instant Pot much easier. Two eggs, sour cream or yogurt, cheese, basil, salt, and pepper are mixed in a bowl. Give each pocket about a tablespoon of this. Each bag must contain one egg and the remaining egg/cream combination. Almost to the top, fill them. They don't need covering.

Fill the pressure cooker with 1 1/2 cups of water. Put the trivet and egg mold into the pot, then shut the lid. Make sure the valve is closed. Hit Pressure Cook (or Manual) to set the time to 2 minutes, then adjust it using the + and - buttons.

Let it be by myself for precisely 1 minute 45 seconds after it beeps to indicate it is completed. After the pin drops, immediately switch the valve to Venting for a rapid release, open the pot, and remove the trivet and egg mold. Place the plate over the mold and invert the gentle egg bites onto it after letting them settle for a minute.

EGG WHITE BREAKFAST BITES

Preparation Time: 20 mins
Cook Time: 25 mins
Total Time: 45 mins

Ingredients

- cooking spray
- 16 oz carton liquid egg whites
- ½ cup low-fat cottage cheese
- ¼ teaspoon garlic powder
- One tablespoon of fresh basil
- ¼ teaspoon salt
- ¼ cup crumbled feta cheese
- ⅛ teaspoon ground black pepper
- 1 cup packed fresh spinach
- ⅓ cup roasted red peppers

Directions

Set the oven to 350 degrees Fahrenheit (175 degrees C). Put cooking spray liberally into a 12-cup muffin pan.

Blend the egg whites, cottage cheese, garlic powder, salt, and pepper in a blender for about 15 seconds or until they are entirely smooth.

In a bowl, mix spinach, roasted red peppers, and basil. Add the egg mixture, then stir it in. Pour a steady amount of the cross, filling each muffin cup to about

3/4 capacity. Put a teaspoon of feta cheese on top of each muffin.

Bake in the oven for 18 to 20 minutes or until the egg white bits are set.

SALSA EGG BITES

Ingredients

- 6 Large Eggs
- ¼ C Shredded Potato
- ½ C Fresh Salsa
- ½ C Shredded Monterey Jack Cheese

Instructions

Preheat oven to 350 degrees. Grease a standard muffin tin with cooking spray.
Press 2 tsp. of shredded potato into the bottom of 6 muffin molds.
In a large bowl, whisk together eggs, then add ¼ C of the whisked eggs into each mold on top of the potatoes.
Spoon a heaping Tablespoon of salsa into each cup, then sprinkle with a light layer of Monterey Jack cheese.
Bake for 20-25 minutes, then allow to sit in the muffin for five minutes before eating.

CHEESY AVOCADO EGG MUFFINS

Ingredients

- 3 Cups Frozen Potatoes O'Brien with Onion & Peppers - thawed
- Olive Oil
- 1 Large Avocado - chopped
- 6 Large Eggs
- 3 Tablespoons Whole Milk
- 1/4 teaspoon Sea Salt
- 1/8 teaspoon Ground Pepper
- 1 Cup Shredded Mild Cheddar Cheese

Instructions

Preheat oven to 375°F. Spray 12 standard muffin tins with nonstick—coat potatoes with a generous amount of olive oil. Transfer potatoes to muffin tins and bake for 25-30 minutes or until light brown.
Remove potatoes from oven and top with chopped avocados.

Lightly beat eggs with milk, salt, and pepper. Pour egg mixture into muffin tins. Top each with shredded cheese. Bake for 15 minutes. Remove and cool for 5 minutes.

Serve with fresh cilantro, Avocados, and hot sauce.

HOUND DOG BITES

Prep Time: 1 hrs
Cook Time: 5 mins
Additional Time: 10 mins
Total Time: 1 hrs 15 mins

Ingredients

- 1 ½ cups packed brown sugar
- 1 cup water
- ¼ cup maple syrup
- 1 (7-ounce) jar marshmallow creme
- 2 cups peanut butter
- 1 ½ pounds chocolate almond bark broken into chunks
- 10-inch flour tortillas
- 2 cups sugar-frosted cornflake cereal divided
- Ten large bananas, or as needed

Directions

Stir the brown sugar, water, and maple syrup in a saucepan until the sugar dissolves. Bring to a boil, then keep the heat to medium-low to maintain heat.
Mix the marshmallow creme with the peanut butter in a large bowl, and pour the brown sugar mixture over the peanut butter mixture.

With an electric mixer, beat the mixture until fluffy. Refrigerate the fluff.

To make the bites, lay a tortilla out on a work surface. Spread a thin layer of peanut butter fluff onto the tortilla, leaving an edge about 1/4 inch wide all the way around, free from the spread.

Sprinkle about 1 1/2 tablespoons of frosted flake cereal over the spread.

Lay a banana along one side of the tortilla; if one banana is too short of reaching the entire length of the tortilla, use 1 1/2 bananas. Tightly roll the tortilla around the banana.

With a sharp serrated knife, cut the roll into 1/2-inch thick slices. Lay the pieces out flat on waxed paper.

In a bowl appropriate for the microwave, place the chocolate almond bark. Microwave for 1 minute, stirring after each 30-second interval until the chocolate coating is smooth and warm (not hot).

Dip the bottom of a slice into the coating, covering about 2/3 of the piece's height. Place the dipped slice coated side down on a sheet of waxed paper to set. Repeat with remaining slices.

Place slices into the refrigerator to chill. Place the remaining cereal flakes in a shallow bowl and lightly crush them.

Dip the other side of the slices into the chocolate coating, and immediately dip the coated area into the crushed flakes. Place the rolls onto waxed paper and flake sides up. Chill the pieces in the refrigerator until the tops have been set up.

BROCCOLI CHEDDAR EGG BITES

Prep time: 10 minutes
Cook time: 12 minutes
Total time: 22 minutes
Yield: 12 muffins

Ingredients

- o seven eggs
- o 1/4 cup whole or 2% milk
- o 1/4 teaspoon salt
- o Pinch of black pepper
- o 1 cup chopped broccoli
- o 1/2 cup shredded sharp cheddar cheese

Instructions

Preheat the oven to 350 degrees.In a large bowl, add the broccoli and one tablespoon of water. Microwave for 1-2 minutes until the broccoli is bright green and softened. Whisk together the milk, eggs, salt, and pepper.

Add steamed broccoli and cheese to the bottom of each silicone muffin cup. Add 2-3 tablespoons of the egg mixture to each muffin cup.

Bake for 22-25 minutes until the egg mixture is set.

Note: You'll need a silicone muffin pan for this recipe

SUN-DRIED TOMATO AND SOUS VIDE EGG BITES

Prep Time: 15 mins
Cook Time: 55 mins
Total Time: 1 hrs 10 mins

Ingredients

- ¼ cup oil-packed sun-dried tomatoes
- one teaspoon of balsamic vinegar
- ⅛ teaspoon garlic powder
- salt and ground black pepper to taste
- six large eggs
- ½ cup cottage cheese
- 2 ounces goat cheese
- two tablespoons of heavy cream
- ½ teaspoon salt
- 6 (4-ounce) mason jars
- cooking spray

Directions

The sous vide immersion cooker should be immersed in a big pot of water. As per the manufactures instructions, set the temperature to 170 degrees F. Tomato oil must be drained, saving 1/2 teaspoon: Put tomatoes in a small bowl after finely chopping them.

Add the vinegar, salt, pepper, garlic powder, and the reserved oil.

Combine by mixing, then put aside.Combine the eggs, cottage cheese, goat cheese, heavy cream, and 1/2 teaspoon salt in a blender. Blend for 15 to 20 seconds or until completely smooth.

BAKED EGG WHITE BITES

Prep Time-5 minutes
Cook Time-25 minutes
Total Time-30 minutes
Servings-6 bites

Ingredients

- Eight egg whites
- ⅓ cup cottage cheese
- ¼ cup bacon bits
- Two tablespoons green onion chopped
- ¼ cup shredded cheddar cheese, optional optional
- salt and pepper

Instructions

In a bowl, separate the egg whites from the yolks. You may save the yolks for another dish, such as French toast or crème brûlée.

Green onion, bacon bits, and cottage cheese should be whisked in. Spoon the batter into a muffin tray that's been well-greased.

Add the cheddar cheese and salt and pepper, if using, to the top. Bake the eggs for 25 minutes at 350°F or until they seem set.

After baking, the bites will puff, though some of that volume will be lost as they cool. Before removing them from the pan, let them cool.

Notes

You may replace four eggs for the eight egg whites asked for in this recipe if you want to use entire eggs rather than only egg whites.

TACO EGG BREAKFAST MUFFINS

Prep Time: 10 minutes
Cook Time: 30 minutes
Resting time: 5 minutes
Total Time: 40 minutes
Servings: 24 muffins

Equipment

- Chefs Knife
- Silicone baking cups

Ingredients

- 1 tsp. Olive oil
- One lb. ground beef, lean
- 1 oz. a packet of taco seasoning, low sodium
- 12 large eggs
- One medium bell pepper, green
- 1/4 cup cilantro, chopped or 1 Tbsp. dried cilantro
- 1 15 oz. can of black beans, low sodium, drained, rinsed

- 15 cherry tomatoes, diced (about 1/2 cup) or 1/2 can of diced tomatoes
- One jalapeño, diced
- 1 cup shredded cheese

Topping ideas: avocado, sour cream, salsa

Instructions

Preheat oven to 350° F. Prepares two cupcake tins by placing them in silicone liners or spraying them with nonstick cooking spray. Set aside.
A medium skillet or frying pan with medium heat is used to heat the olive oil. After adding, cook the ground beef until it is no longer pink. Mix one packet of taco seasoning into the prepared food before setting it aside.

In a bowl, crack the eggs and mix them. Next, include the cheese, tomatoes, black beans, bell pepper, cilantro, jalapeno, and ground meat. Mix until thoroughly blended.
Scoop the egg mixture into the prepared cupcake tin, filling each about ¾ way. Repeat until the mixture is finished (will make 24 muffins).

Bake in the oven for 27-30 minutes or until eggs are cooked. Let cool slightly and then enjoy as is or with sour cream, avocado chunks, and salsa on top!

Notes

Make these for meal prep: store them in an airtight container in the refrigerator, then reheat them in the microwave or oven just before serving. They are great for busy mornings, back to school, or brunch!

CENTURY EGG WITH SILKEN TOFU

Prep Time-5 mins
Active Time-5 mins
Total Time-10 mins
Yield: 4 people

Materials

- 1 pack of silken tofu 750g
- 3 Century Egg sliced
- Four cloves of garlic chopped
- Two stalks of green onion chopped
- 2-3 red chili chopped (optional)
- 1 tsp sugar
- Two tablespoons of vegetarian oyster sauce
- 1.5 tablespoon soy sauce
- ½ tablespoon sesame oil
- Three tablespoons oil
- Cilantro to garnish

Instructions

Heat three tablespoons of heated oil to make the sauce.

Combine chopped green onion, garlic, and red chili in a bowl. Pour hot oil over the ingredients in a thin layer. Add a few drops each of soy sauce, sesame oil, vegetarian oyster sauce, and sugar. Combine thoroughly, then stop.

Place the silken tofu in the center of the platter to offer the dish. Place the century eggs all over the tofu before adding the sauce and cilantro as finishing touches.

Notes

If you're nervous since it's your first time, try heating the Egg for 5 minutes. The taste will be softer, and the yolk inside will become less runny after cooking.

INSTANT POT EGG BITES

Prep time-10 mins
Cook time-25 mins
Total time-35 mins
Servings-7 servings

Ingredients

- Three large eggs

- 1/4 cup cottage cheese
- 1/4 cup soft cheese, like cream cheese, Brie, Boursin, or Laughing Cow
- 1/2 cup chopped mix-ins, like cooked meats and raw or cooked vegetables
- 1/2 cup shredded cheese, such as cheddar, Monterey jack, or mozzarella

Method

Mix the cheeses and eggs: Place the cottage cheese, soft cheese, and eggs in a blender. Mix at medium speed until smooth, about 30 seconds.

Mix-ins: Spoon the thoroughly combined egg mixture into a bowl. Stir in the shredded cheese and chopped mix-ins after adding them.

Fill the molds: Lightly lubricate a silicone egg mold with oil or nonstick cooking spray before filling each hole with 1/4 cup of the mixture. Clean up any drips.

Get the pressure cooker prepared:

Fill the Instant Pot or electric pressure cooker with 1 cup of water. Place an 8-inch parchment ring or aluminum foil on top of the egg mold to prevent moisture from falling onto the bites while they cook. Gently move the egg mold to the wire steam rack.

Lift the egg mold into the pot while holding the handles of the steam rack. Secure the pressure cooker's cover before cooking the eggs under low pressure. A pressure regulator must be adjusted to the "Sealing" position. Adjust the time to 8 minutes at low pressure after selecting the "Pressure Cook" or "Manual" program. The pressure cooker will reach its maximum pressure in around 10 minutes. After it has reached its highest point, cook time begins.

Note:

If your pressure cooker doesn't have a low-pressure setting, use the "Pressure Cook" or "Manual" setting for 8 minutes. Just making one layer of egg bits at a time is our advice. The "Steam" feature may also be set for 10 minutes.

Let the pressure relax for five minutes after the timer goes off naturally. Then, quickly release the pressure by switching the pressure release knob from "Sealing" to "Venting." The pressure won't dissipate for a minute or two.

The egg bits must be taken out of the pressure cooker. Grab the ends of the wire rack while wearing heatproof mittens to remove the egg bite mold from the pot. After removing the parchment, allow the bites to cool for around two minutes (they will deflate a bit as they cool). Use a spoon to remove the edges from the mold and place them in a serving dish.

Egg bits must be served warm, either on their own or with toast or a bed of mixed greens.

You may store them in a container with a tight lid in the refrigerator for up to 3 days. Before serving, reheat in the microwave for only a little time (up to 25 seconds, depending on your microwave's power).

FIESTA EGG BITES

Prep Time: 10 minutes
Cook Time: 20 minutes
Total Time: 30 minutes
Servings: 6

Ingredients

- 1/2 cup Diced Tomatoes from a 14.5 oz can
- 1 TBSP butter
- 1/2 cup diced sweet peppers
- 1/4 cup diced yellow onion
- 2 tsp taco seasoning
- Seven large eggs
- 2 TBSP milk
- 1 cup grated cheddar or taco blend cheese

Instructions

Heat oven to 350 degrees F. Use Pam Baking Spray to spray a tiny muffin tray.

Pour one-half of the can of chopped tomatoes into a colander and allow the liquid to dry. Put the butter in a small saucepan and heat it over medium heat. Heat the butter, then add the peppers and onion and simmer for 7-8 minutes, or until tender. Add taco spice to a bowl and set away.

While peppers are cooking, firmly mix together eggs and milk. Whisk in half of the shredded cheese and continue whisking.

Incorporate a few peppers into each muffin cup. (About one-half teaspoon), Measure out 1/2 cup of tomatoes from the amount that has been drained. Each muffin cup should get a little amount of chopped tomatoes. (about 1 teaspoon), Before nearly completely filling each muffin cup with the egg mixture, it should be whisked again. Sprinkle the remaining cheese in each muffin cup.

Bake for 17-20 minutes, until egg bits are puffed up. Turn off the heat. Let egg bites to cool for 5 minutes, then remove them from the muffin tray using a thin knife, if necessary.

Enjoy! Keep leftovers in a container that is airtight. Egg Bites may be frozen and later reheated.

BACON AND EGG BITES

Preparation time less than 30 mins
Cooking time-10 to 30 mins
Serves 6

Ingredients

- 12 bacon medallions
- 12 free-range eggs
- 12 small cherry tomatoes, halved
- freshly ground black pepper
- Six slices of bread to serve
- knob of butter to spread

Method

A muffin pan with 12 holes must be lightly greased and the oven set at 220 C.

Roll out the bacon medallions with a rolling pin after placing them between two sheets of cling film. Make a case out of them by putting them within the muffin tray.

Add two tomato halves on top of each cracked Egg, sprinkle with black pepper, then top with a bacon case. The bacon and Egg must bake for 10 minutes in the oven to cook through. Cook your Egg for 15 minutes if you want it well done.

After the bread is sufficiently toasted, gently butter it. Give each guest two egg bites and a piece of bread.

BAKED EGG MUFFINS

Prep Time-10 minutes
Cook Time-20 minutes
Servings-12 cups

Ingredients

- Six large eggs
- 1 cup egg whites or another six eggs
- 1/2 teaspoon sea salt
- 1/2 teaspoon ground pepper
- One teaspoon of olive oil
- 1/2 orange bell pepper, chopped
- 1/2 cup yellow onion, chopped
- 1 cup broccoli, chopped into small pieces
- 1 cup mushrooms, sliced
- 1/3 cup crumbled feta
- 2 Tablespoons fresh parsley
- cooking spray, I use coconut oil

Instructions

Preheat: Preheat to 375 degrees Fahrenheit.

Muffin pan preparation: Spray cooking spray or line the twelve-cup muffin tray with silicone baking cups. To be on the safe side, I sprayed the silicone baking cups.

Eggs must be whisked together after being added to a large bowl with egg whites. Add salt and pepper to taste.
To sauté vegetables, heat one teaspoon of oil in a pan over medium heat. When the bell pepper, onion, broccoli, and mushrooms are pretty soft, and the onions are fragrant, add the chopped vegetables and simmer for 5–6 minutes.

Mix-ins: Place steamed vegetables in the bowl holding the whisked eggs. Mix thoroughly before adding the feta and parsley.

Split the mixture: Evenly pour the egg mixture into the muffin tins. I sprayed each one using a measuring cup that held 1/3 cup.

Bake: Bake the egg cups for 17 to 20 minutes, until they are no longer jiggly and a toothpick inserted into one comes out clean. Let cups cool before drinking.

STARBUCKS EGG BITES

Servings-6
Prep time-5 minutes
Cooking time-30minutes

Ingredients

- Five eggs
- Nonstick spray or butter
- 1 cup shredded cheese
- 1 cup whole-fat cottage cheese
- Pinch of salt
- Pinch of pepper
- 1 tsp olive oil
- Three strips of bacon

Directions

Your oven needs to be preheated to 340°F first. Take your muffin tin and oil, or spray 6 cups with nonstick spray while the oven is preheating.

In a sizeable bowl, add the eggs, and whisk the mixture well. Add salt, pepper, and cheese to the cottage cheese. All of the ingredients should be well combined after pounding.

Equally, distribute the ingredients among your six muffin tins. After that, bake for 30 minutes.
Bake your Starbucks egg pieces while a skillet is heated on medium-low heat.Include olive oil to the pan and add three bacon rashers. Fry the bacon on each side

until it is crispy and sizzling for about 4 minutes. Next, please remove the bacon and let it cool on some towels.

Remove the egg bites from the oven when they are fluffy and golden, which should occur after 30 minutes. Equally, distribute the bacon bits on top of the egg bites.

Enjoy after cooking.

JALAPEÑO POPPER BREAKFAST EGG MUFFINS

Prep Time: 8 mins
Cook Time: 15 minutes
Total Time: 22 minutes

Ingredients

- Ten large eggs
- One teaspoon of sea salt or to taste
- 1/4 teaspoon black pepper or to taste
- 1/2 teaspoon garlic powder
- 1/2 teaspoon onion powder
- 3-4 jalapeño peppers de-seeded and chopped
- 1/3 cup cream cheese softened
- 1/2 cup cheddar cheese shredded
- 1/3 cup bacon cooked crumbled

Instructions

Set the oven to 400 F. Use a silicone muffin pan or a 12-count tin lined with silicone liners. Or, use nonstick cooking spray to coat a standard muffin pan. Set aside. Crack eggs into a big mixing bowl and whisk in salt and black pepper.

Mix the other ingredients and distribute evenly among the muffin cups, filling each one approximately 2/3 full. Put cheese on top.

In each muffin cup, place a few jalapeno slices on top. Bake in a preheated oven for 12 to 17 minutes or until set.

PESTO EGG BITES

Prep Time-5 min
Cook time-10 min
Yield -12 servings

Ingredients

- Cooking spray
- 6 Egg land's Best eggs
- 1/4 cup fat-free feta or goat cheese
- 18 cherry tomatoes, quartered
- Two tablespoons of fat-free milk
- 1 1/2 tablespoons refrigerated pesto
- 1/2 teaspoon kosher salt
- 1/4 teaspoon freshly ground black pepper

Preparation

Preheat oven to 350 degrees Fahrenheit. Coat a mini-muffin pan for 24 servings with cooking spray.

Distribute the tomato quarters among the muffin cups, and sprinkle each with 1/2 teaspoon of feta or goat cheese.
In a large glass measuring cup or basin, crack eggs. Whisk together milk, pesto, salt, and pepper.

Pour mixture into muffin tins evenly. Bake for 10 minutes at 350°F or until the muffins are done. Please keep away from the muffins from the pan and wait for them cool on a wire rack for two to three minutes.

VEGGIE AND QUINOA EGG BITES

Prep time-5 minutes
Cook time-15-20 minutes
Yield-12 egg bites

Ingredients

- 2 cups cooked quinoa
- 2 cups cheddar cheese, shredded
- 2 cups of cooked veggies of your choice
- 2 Nellie's Free Range Eggs
- One teaspoon of kosher salt

Directions

Preheat oven to 350F. Add cooking spray to a tiny muffin tray.

In a deep bowl, mix all ingredients until well combined. Divide the mixture evenly in the mini muffin pan. Make sure you press down to pack it in firmly.

Bake mini muffins for 15-20 minutes until golden brown and crispy. Note: every oven is different.My quinoa bites took about 20 minutes to get brown and crispy.

Enjoy!

CHICKEN TACO EGG MINI MUFFINS

Preparation Time: 25 mins
Cook Time: 25 mins
Total Time: 50 mins

Ingredients

- One tablespoon of olive oil
- ⅓ pound ground chicken
- One tablespoon of taco seasoning
- Six large eggs, beaten
- 1 cup shredded Cheddar cheese
- ½ cup milk
- ½ red bell pepper, finely chopped

- One shallot, finely chopped
- ¼ cup finely chopped mushrooms
- Two tablespoons finely chopped chives
- ½ jalapeno pepper, finely chopped
- One tablespoon of hot sauce (Optional)
- salt and ground black pepper to taste

Directions

Heat a medium skillet over medium-high heat. Add oil. Add chicken and cook until browned, 5 to 7 minutes. Mix in taco seasoning. Remove from heat and set aside.

Set the oven to 350 degrees Fahrenheit (175 degrees C). A big bowl should include the following ingredients: eggs, Cheddar cheese, milk, red bell pepper, shallot, mushrooms, chives, jalapeño, spicy sauce, salt, and pepper. Add the chicken mixture that has cooled.
Fill each cup in the nonstick small muffin pans 3/4 full with the mixture.

Around 18 minutes should pass in the oven before the eggs are set.

PRESSURE COOKER CORN DOG BITES

Prep Time10 minutes
Cook Time9 minutes
Total Time19 minutes
Servings-14

Ingredients

- Four hot dogs cut into 4ths
- 1 1/4 c flour
- 3/4 c cornmeal
- 1/4 c sugar
- 2 tsp baking powder
- 1/2 tsp salt
- 1 c milk
- One egg
- 1/4 c oil optional, have with or without it when I was out, and it turned out similarly

Instructions

Combine the dry ingredients for the cornbread, then mix in the milk, oil, and egg. Spray nonstick spray to the interior of your egg mold (well). Put the cornbread mixture halfway inside each pocket.
Cut each hot dog into four equal pieces, then place one element in the center of each pitcher hole.

Cover the fiber egg mold. Your pressure cooker should contain 1.5 c of water. Egg mold must be placed on a trivet with handles and lowered into the pot.

Shut the lid and steam valve, then set the timer for 9 minutes on high pressure. Then give the steam five minutes to release naturally. After that, let off some more steam.
To ensure they stay intact when you pop them out of the form, remove the foil right away and let them cool in the mold for 3–4 minutes.

Next, turn it over and gently press the bottom pockets to release each corn dog bite.

OLIVE OIL-FRIED EGG

Yield: 4 eggs

Ingredients

- Three tablespoons extra-virgin olive oil
- Four eggs
- Kosher salt and black pepper

Preparation

Heat the olive oil to sea ripples in a medium (10-inch) cast-iron or non-stick pan over medium-high heat. (This might take between two and two and a half minutes.

The eggs are put into the pan. Open the egg's shell near the oil (not from above) and slowly let the egg pour out to reduce splatters and spread. The eggs should be left unattended for 2 to 3 minutes or until the rims are golden brown.

Carefully tilt the pan in your direction, scoop up some oil, and baste only the yolk's edges and whites for approximately a minute or until the whites are set. Use a spoon or slotted spatula to transfer the eggs to plates after turning off the heat and seasoning them with salt and pepper.

This technique for preparing fried eggs falls midway between traditional sunny side up and Spanish fried eggs: The whites are set and have crispy golde borders, but the yolk is still fluid. The eggs are prepared in a thin coating of sizzling-hot oil to create this contrast in textures. Although the recipe calls for four eggs, it may be made with any number.

Wait to touch the eggs until the bottoms and edges are lacy and crisp. When that happens, pour some oil over the egg whites and fry them until done. The yolk is still unfilled and waiting to be guzzled with toast, potatoes, or yogurt.

SIZZLING BALUT

Prep Time: 15 mins
Cook Time: 20 mins
Total Time: 35 mins

Ingredients

- Four baluts, cooked and peeled
- 1/4 cup flour
- 1/4 cup canola oil
- Two shallots, peeled and chopped
- Two cloves garlic, peeled and minced
- One thumb-size ginger, peeled and minced
- 3 Thai chili peppers, minced
- 1/2 small red bell pepper, seeded and chopped
- One tablespoon of soy sauce
- Three tablespoons of oyster sauce
- 1/4 cup water

- One tablespoon of green onions, chopped
- pepper to taste

Instructions

Balut must be lightly flour-dredged in a shallow dish. A giant skillet with medium heat is used to heat the oil. Cook the balut until gently browned, flipping it once or twice. After turning off the heat, dry the pan with paper towels.

Remove everything except about one tablespoon of the oil from the pan. Add the bell pepper, chili peppers, ginger, garlic, and shallots. Turn the heat down while often stirring until aromatic and soft.

Soy sauce, oyster sauce, and water should be combined in a bowl. Blend after thoroughly mixing. Stir in the pan, then bring to a boil. After the balut is heated and the sauce has thickened, add it and continue to cook, gently turning to cover it with sauce. To taste, add pepper to the dish.
Remove from pan and place on sizzling plates. Serve hot with green onions as a garnish.

Notes

To help maintain heat, serve the balut with spicy sauce on sizzling metal plates. Before serving, briefly warm the plates in the oven or stovetop.

BRIK-STYLE EGGS

Hands-On: 45 mins
Total: 55 mins
Yield: Serves 4

Ingredients

Harissa:
- One teaspoon of caraway seeds
- One teaspoon of cumin seeds
- One teaspoon of ground ancho chile pepper
- ¾ cup chopped bottled roasted red bell peppers
- Two tablespoons water
- ½ teaspoon sugar
- One garlic clove, crushed

Brik:
- About 12 oz cubed Yukon gold potato
- Two teaspoons of olive oil
- ½ teaspoon ground turmeric
- ¼ teaspoon kosher salt
- ⅛ teaspoon ground red pepper (optional)
- ¼ cup chopped fresh parsley
- ⅓ cup thinly sliced green onions
- 13 x 18-inch sheets of frozen phyllo dough
- Cooking spray
- Four large eggs, chilled
- 2 oz feta cheese, crumbled (about 1/2 cup)
- ¼ teaspoon black pepper
- One large egg white

- One teaspoon water
- ¼ cup chopped fresh cilantro

Directions

Caraway and cumin seeds must be cooked for one minute while stirring in a small skillet over medium-high heat to make harissa. Blend the seed mixture, ancho chile pepper, and the following four ingredients until smooth.

Put the potatoes in a pot, add the water, and boil to make a brik. Simmer for 10 minutes, or until just tender, on reduced heat. Drain.

Set the oven to 450 degrees.Large non-stick skillet with oil heated to medium-high heat; swirl to coat. When the edges are crisp, add the potatoes, turmeric, salt, and ground red pepper (if using). Sauté for 6 minutes. Stirring regularly, simmer for 2 minutes after adding the parsley and green onions.Keep away from heat and let cool for five minutes.

One sheet of phyllo dough must be placed on a large cutting board or work surface. The cooking spray must be applied to the remaining phyllo to avoid drying. Partially the sheet is like a book. Spray some cooking spray on the phyllo's bottom third (the narrow end should face you). Upfold the bottom third. Make an egg nest by placing 1/4 of the potatoes in the center of the bottom (folded) third of the phyllo. In the center of the potatoes, crack one egg. Top the egg with 1/4 of the feta. Add some black pepper. Fold in the sides to make a package by folding the top third of the phyllo over the egg, potatoes, and cheese. A packet must be put on a baking sheet with cooking spray. Repeat is required with the rest of the phyllo, potatoes, eggs, cheese, and black pepper. With a whisk, combine the egg white and one teaspoon of water in a small bowl. Brush the egg white mixture on the phyllo packets. Bake for 9 minutes at 450 degrees or until crisp and golden. Sprinkle cilantro over the brik after equally distributing the harissa.

CHINESE STEAMED EGGS

Prep: 3 minutes
Cook: 10 minutes
Total: 13 minutes
Servings: 2

Ingredients

- Two eggs - beaten
- 1 pinch salt
- Warm water
- One teaspoon chive
- Two teaspoons of light soy sauce
- Two drops of sesame oil
- Extra garnish (optional)
- Prawns - peeled and deveined
- Asparagus & carrot

Instructions

Warm water ought to be added to the beaten eggs. Stir well after adding salt.

Pour the mixture into two little serving bowls through a sieve. If using, sprinkle chive on top.
Bowls are covered with cling film. Pierce to make space for the steam to vent.

10 to 12 minutes of gentle boiling (place the bowls in when the water starts to boil).
Sesame oil and light soy sauce are used to season (if you wish, cut through the curd several times to let the sauce penetrate). Serve warm.
If adding garnish, steam the egg as usual for 7 minutes before adding the prawns and vegetables. Add three more minutes of boiling.

NOTES

1. The volume of the egg water mixture should be about 1:2. For instance, two medium-sized beaten eggs measure around 100ml. Thus 200ml of water is required.
2. The water's ideal temperature is 45°C (113°F). This can be done by combining hot and tap water in equal parts.

SHIRRED EGGS

Prep Time: 10 mins
Cook Time: 15 mins
Total Time: 25 mins

Ingredients

- ¼ teaspoon softened butter
- Two teaspoons of heavy cream
- Two eggs
- salt and pepper to taste
- One teaspoon of minced fresh chives
- One teaspoon of grated Parmesan cheese

Directions

Set oven to 325 degrees Fahrenheit (165 degrees C).

Butter must be applied to a 6-ounce ramekin's inside.
Before cracking the eggs on top of the cream without
breaking the yolks, pour the cream into the ramekin.
Place the yolks in the center of the ramekin using a
spoon, and then top with Parmesan, chives, salt, and
pepper.
Bake in a preheated oven for 12 to 15 minutes or until
the egg whites are set, but the yolks are still liquid.
After taking it out of the oven, let it rest for two to three
minutes before serving.

CREAMED EGGS ON TOAST

Prep Time: 20 mins
Cook Time: 5 mins
Total Time: 25 mins

Ingredients

- 12 hard-cooked eggs, peeled
- ¼ cup butter
- ½ cup all-purpose flour
- 3 cups milk
- One tablespoon of chicken bouillon granules
- Six slices white bread, lightly toasted
- salt and white pepper to taste

Directions

Sort the egg yolks and whites separately. Using a fork, mash the egg yolks after placing them in a bowl. The egg whites must be finely chopped and left aside.

In a pot on medium heat, melt the butter. Add flour and mix until smooth. Stir continuously while adding the milk and chicken bouillon gradually to prevent lumps from developing until the mixture boils. Include the egg yolks and stir to combine. Add egg whites and mix. Add salt and white pepper to the stew and serve over toast.

BACON, EGG & CHEESE QUICHE

Prep-30 mins
Bake-45 to 55 mins
Total-1 hr 25 mins

Ingredients

Filling

- 3/4 pound (340g) bacon
- 340g yellow onion, peeled
- Two tablespoons (28g) butter
- salt and pepper
- 170g heavy cream
- 57g milk
- Six large eggs
- 170g grated Cabot Alpine Cheddar
- 1/4 teaspoon salt
- 1/4 teaspoon black pepper
- Take your baking to the next level: virtual classes

Instructions

Turn the oven on to 375°F.
Roll the prepared pie dough into a 12-inch circle for the
crust (to fit a 9" pie pan). Using a fork, stab it all over.
The crust must be cooked for 10 minutes, taken out,
and let to cool.

Creating the filling In a frying pan, cook the bacon until crisp. On a platter covered with towels, let it cool. When it has fantastic, roughly slice it.

Cut the onion into medium-sized (about 1/2") dice. Over medium heat, melt the butter and add the onion to the pan. Use salt and pepper to taste to season. Sauté the onion until it has softened and is just beginning to turn brown. It is taken off the stove and put aside.

HOW TO MAKE SCRAMBLED EGGS

Prep Time: 2 mins
Cook Time: 3 mins
Total Time: 5 mins
Serves 1 to 2

Ingredients

- Three large eggs
- Extra-virgin olive oil
- Sea salt and fresh black pepper
- One teaspoon milk, plant milk
- Chopped fresh chives

Instructions

Add the milk or water to the medium bowl with the broken eggs. Stir until the mixture is mixed and streaks of egg white are gone completely.

Melt some butter in a small non-stick skillet or brush some olive oil in the pan. Heat to a moderate. The eggs must be poured in and left to simmer for a little while without being stirred. Drag a rubber spatula across the pan's bottom to create big, soft curds of scrambled eggs.

Folding and stir the eggs every few seconds as you fry them over medium-low heat. To create additional curds and stop any portion of the eggs from drying out, constantly scrape the spatula along the bottom and edges of the pan.

Remove the pan from the heat when the eggs are mostly set but still have some liquid egg. Garnish with finely chopped fresh chives and season with salt & pepper to taste.

BASIC OMELET RECIPE

Prep:5 mins
Cook:5 mins
Serves 1

Ingredients

- Three eggs, beaten
- 1 tsp sunflower oil
- 1 tsp butter

Method

Salt and pepper the beaten eggs generously. Heat the oil and butter over medium-low heat in a non-stick frying pan until the butter has melted and is foaming. Pour the eggs into the pan, then tilt it just a bit from side to side to give the eggs room to swirl and thoroughly coat the pan's surface. After letting the mixture cook for about 20 seconds, use a spatula to make a line across the middle.

To re-fill the pan with the runny egg, tilt it again. Continue this a couple more times until the egg is almost set.

The omelet may now be filled with anything you like, including grated cheese, sliced ham, fresh herbs, sautéed mushrooms, and smoked salmon. Spread the filling on top of the omelet and use a new spatula to fold it in half gently. To serve, slide onto a plate.

CONCLUSION

In conclusion, egg bites are a popular and versatile food that can be enjoyed in various ways. These bite-sized treats are often made with eggs, cheese, and other ingredients and can be cooked in multiple ways, including in the oven or sous vide machine. Egg bites are an excellent choice for breakfast, lunch, or a snack, as they are high in protein and easily customized to suit individual tastes and preferences. Whether you prefer classic egg and cheese bites or more exotic flavors like bacon and avocado, egg bites are delicious and satisfying food that can be enjoyed anytime. Overall, egg bites are a tasty and convenient food that will surely be a hit with food lovers everywhere.

TIPS AND TRICKS

Egg bites are a delicious and convenient breakfast or snack option you can easily make at home. Here are some advice and tricks to help you make perfect egg bites every time:

Use a silicone mold: Silicone molds are great for making egg bites because they are flexible and non-stick, making it easy to remove the egg bites without them sticking to the sides. You can find silicone molds in various shapes and sizes, so you can select one that fits your needs.

Preheat the oven: It's important to preheat the oven before baking the egg bites. This will assure that they cook evenly and prevent them from being undercooked or overcooked.

Use a blender: To ensure that the egg bites have a smooth and creamy texture, it's best to use a blender to mix the ingredients. This will also help incorporate air into the mixture, making the egg bites light and fluffy.

Add cheese: Adding cheese to the egg mixture will give the egg bites extra flavor and help to keep them moist. You can use any cheese, such as cheddar, feta, or mozzarella.

Customize the ingredients: Add any ingredients you like to the egg bites, such as cooked bacon, spinach, mushrooms, or onions. Make sure you chop them into small pieces so they cook evenly.

Use a water bath: To prevent the egg bites from getting too dry, you can bake them in a water bath. Place the silicone mold in a larger baking dish filled with about an inch of hot water before baking.

Let them cool: Once the egg bites are done, it's essential to let them cool for a few minutes before removing them from the mold. This will help them set and make it easier to remove them without breaking them.

You can make perfect egg bites every time by following these suggestions and tricks.

Enjoy!

To reheat egg bites and keep them tasting fresh and delicious, you can follow these steps:

1. Preheat your oven to 175°C.
2. Remove the egg bites from the refrigerator and place them on a baking sheet.
3. Cover the egg bites loosely with aluminum foil to prevent them from drying.
4. Put the required baking sheet in the oven and bake for 10-15 minutes.
5. Check the egg bites for doneness. They should be hot all the way through.
6. If the egg bites need more time, continue to heat them in 5-minute increments, checking for doneness after each interval.
7. Once the egg bites are heated through, extract them from the oven and wait to cool for a few minutes before serving.

Alternatively, you can reheat the egg bites in the microwave, which may cause them to become rubbery and overcooked. If you use the microwave, place the egg bites on a microwave-safe plate and heat on high for 30-second intervals, checking for doneness after each break.

Thank you for Choosing this book

THE END

Made in the USA
Las Vegas, NV
07 January 2024

84018646R00046